Natchiq Grows Up

NATCHIQ GROWS UP

The Story of a Ringed Seal Pup and Her Changing Home

Donna D. W. Hauser, Kathryn J. Frost, and Alex V. Whiting
with contributions from John Goodwin, Cyrus Harris, and Pearl Goodwin
Illustrations by Heather McFarland

University of Alaska Press

FAIRBANKS

Published by University of Alaska Press
An imprint of University Press of Colorado
1580 North Logan Street, Suite 660
PMB 39883
Denver, Colorado 80203-1942

 The University Press of Colorado is a proud member of Association of University Presses.

The University Press of Colorado is a cooperative publishing enterprise supported, in part, by Adams State University, Colorado State University, Fort Lewis College, Metropolitan State University of Denver, University of Alaska Fairbanks, University of Colorado, University of Denver, University of Northern Colorado, University of Wyoming, Utah State University, and Western Colorado University.

∞ This paper meets the requirements of the ANSI/NISO Z39.48-1992 (Permanence of Paper).

ISBN: 978-1-64642-538-9 (hardcover)
ISBN: 978-1-64642-539-6 (paperback)
ISBN: 978-1-64642-540-2 (ebook)
https://doi.org/10.5876/9781646425402

Library of Congress Cataloging-in-Publication Data

Names: Hauser, Donna D. W., author. | Frost, Kathryn J., author. | Whiting, Alex V., author. | Goodwin, John (Hunter), contributor. | Harris, Cyrus (Hunter), contributor. | Goodwin, Pearl, contributor. | McFarland, Heather, illustrator.
Title: Natchiq grows up : the story of a ringed seal pup and her changing home / Donna D. W. Hauser, Kathryn J. Frost, Alex V. Whiting ; with contributions from John Goodwin, Cyrus Harris, Pearl Goodwin ; illustrations by Heather McFarland.
Description: Fairbanks : University of Alaska Press, [2023] | Audience: Ages 5–11 | Audience: Grades 2–3
Identifiers: LCCN 2023033393 (print) | LCCN 2023033394 (ebook) | ISBN 9781646425389 (hardcover) | ISBN 9781646425396 (paperback) | ISBN 9781646425402 (ebook)
Subjects: LCSH: Ringed seal—Alaska—Kotzebue Sound—Juvenile literature. | Ringed seal—Life cycles—Alaska—Kotzebue Sound—Juvenile literature. | Ringed seal—Infancy—Alaska—Kotzebue Sound—Juvenile literature. | Ringed seal—Habitations—Alaska—Kotzebue Sound—Juvenile literature. | Ringed seal—Habitat—Alaska—Kotzebue Sound—Juvenile literature.
Classification: LCC QL737.P64 H38 2023 (print) | LCC QL737.P64 (ebook) | DDC 599.79/2—dc23/eng/20230911
LC record available at https://lccn.loc.gov/2023033393
LC ebook record available at https://lccn.loc.gov/2023033394

Cover and interior design by Krista West.
Cover photo: Ringed seal near Kotzebue, Alaska. Photo by Michael Cameron (NOAA permit 15126).
Cover illustration: sculptured shrimp by Alex V. Whiting.
Opening photo: Ice forming in front of Kotzebue in November 2019. Photo by Donna D. W. Hauser.

We acknowledge the Alaska Native nations upon whose ancestral lands the University of Alaska resides.

INDIGENOUS KNOWLEDGE

In Kotzebue, research for this book happened in cooperation with—and on the lands of— the Qikiqtaġruŋmiut (the people of Kotzebue).

Seal tagging crew in Kotzebue Sound, October 2008. Pictured from front to back, left side row: Doc Harris, John Goodwin, Kathryn Frost, Jeff Barger. Middle holding seal hind flippers: Edward Ahyakak. Front to back, right side: Grover Harris, Grover Harris Jr., Pearl Goodwin.
JUSTIN CRAWFORD
(NOAA PERMIT 358-1787-02)

Ringed seal pup in Kotzebue Sound, May 2011.
MICHAEL CAMERON (NOAA PERMIT 15126)

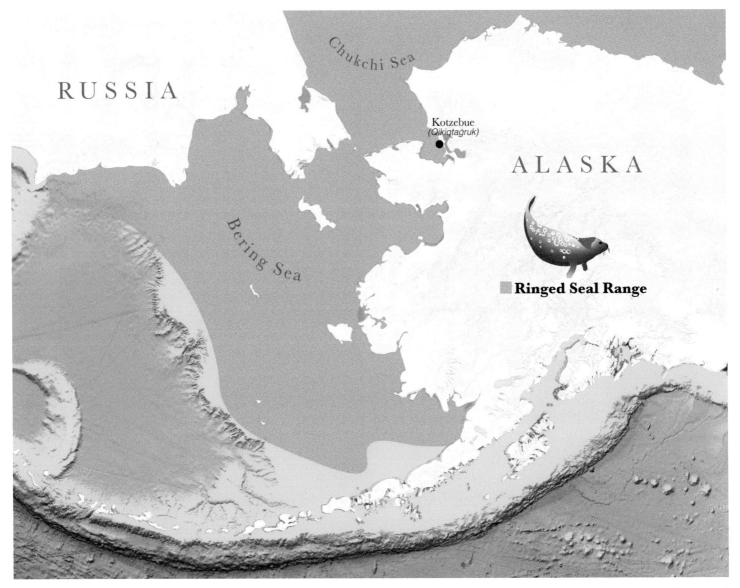

Ringed seals have a wide geographic distribution across the circumpolar arctic and subarctic. Scientists estimate there are more than three million ringed seals worldwide. Their scientific name is Pusa hispida.

MAP BY HEATHER MCFARLAND

Ringed seals are the smallest and most common seal found in Alaska's northern seas.

In fact, ringed seals are one of the most abundant marine mammals found in all of the Arctic regions of the world.

This is the story of a fluffy white ringed seal pup called Natchiq, her mom Siku, and their changing home on the Arctic sea ice.

A ringed seal called Natchiq is born one bright April morning in a cozy snow cave called a lair.

(Facing page) Ringed seal pups are born with dense white fur, called "lanugo," for warmth. Lanugo works like a down coat and provides good insulation against the cold. Pups nurse from their mother for four to six weeks and grow a thick layer of blubber before shedding their lanugo.
LLOYD LOWRY

INDIGENOUS KNOWLEDGE

The Alaska Native people of Kotzebue (the Iñupiaq nation of the Qikiqtaġruŋmiut) have depended on ringed seals for food, fuel, and clothing for thousands of years.

Ringed seals are part of the culture of Indigenous Peoples across the Arctic.

Roswell Schaeffer searching for seals on the spring ice in Kotzebue Sound.
DONNA D.W. HAUSER

LIFE OF A LAIR

STEP 1: Ringed seals find cracks and dig holes in the sea ice to use as breathing holes, which they keep open using their front flipper claws and teeth as the ice grows thicker and the snow becomes deeper during the long Arctic winter.

The ice can grow over six feet thick, and the breathing holes can become cone shaped with just a small opening at the top of the ice.

DRAWING BY HEATHER MCFARLAND

Natchiq's mom, Siku, built the lair so that her pup could be born safely.

The lair began as one of Siku's breathing holes.

Siku dug into the hard-packed snowdrift with her front-flipper claws.

The breathing hole is now a cozy cave with a snowy roof and an icy floor.

SEAL SCIENCE

Long ago, in the winter of 1983, a group of scientists wanted to learn more about ringed seal lairs—the snow-cave homes that seals build on the ice each winter.

✦ How deep is the snow where seals make their homes?
✦ How big are the lairs?
✦ How close together are the lairs?

The scientists' camp on the sea ice in Kotzebue Sound, spring 1983.
KATHRYN J. FROST

Arctic fox and polar bears are two of the most common ringed seal predators.
LLOYD PIKOK JR.

TIĜIGANNIAQ IS THE IÑUPIAQ WORD FOR ARCTIC FOX.

NANUQ IS THE IÑUPIAQ WORD FOR POLAR BEAR.

The lair keeps the ringed seal mom and pup safe from the strong Arctic winds, cold temperatures, and predators like foxes and polar bears.

LIFE OF A LAIR

STEP 2: The ringed seal enlarges the breathing hole so that she can fit her body through the hole. She creates a snow cave next to the hole that is just large enough to fit her.

The ringed seal rests in her snow cave under a thick blanket of snow that grows deeper as the winter continues. She fits snugly in her snow-cave lair, ready to give birth to a pup in early April. The breathing hole is the seal's entrance and exit from the cave to the ocean.

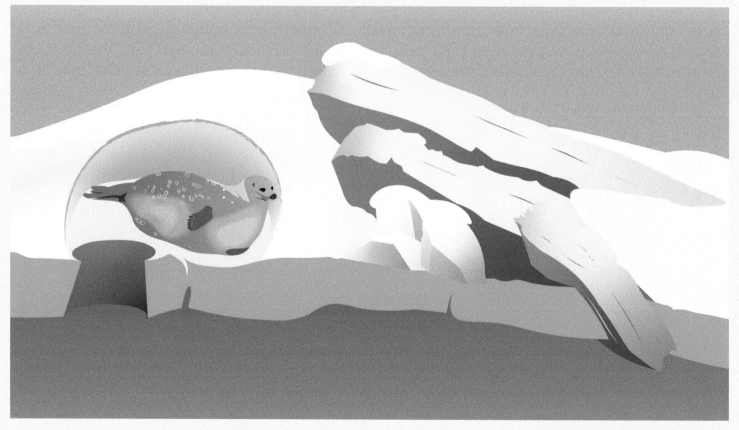

DRAWING BY HEATHER McFARLAND

Ringed seals are marine mammals that breathe air just like other mammals.

Scattered about the ice and inside lairs are breathing holes: doors from the surface of the ice into the ocean.

Inside Natchiq's lair there is a breathing hole.

Cyrus Harris and Donna Hauser discuss ringed seals and sea ice conditions, spring 2018.
SARAH BETCHER

INDIGENOUS KNOWLEDGE: CYRUS HARRIS

Elder Cyrus Harris knows the importance of marine mammals, like ringed seals, to coastal Iñupiat.

"First, the most important reason that people settled on the coast was the importance of sea mammals for clothing and food. Once the animals are processed and the meat is stored in oil, you have a reliable food source for many months.

"For example, you might process the animals in June and consume the products during the winter. Once it is properly processed and stored, for us it is like fast food, a ready-to-eat meal. The oil also goes good with all of our wild game and fish.

"When we are traveling for long distances out in the country and we don't have a lot of room for stuff, one of the easiest things to take with us is the meat in oil products for food. In many situations when times get hard to gather meat and fish in the winter, we always have a supply of dried seal meat and oil to survive off of.

"The skin of the ringed seal can be used in many ways: to make parka, pants, maklaks, hats, gloves. You can dress yourself all in seal-skin clothing that is far superior to Western-made clothes. Back in the old days, the seal skin was made into storage containers (*pokes*) to store food products and oil that was preserved and put aside for our winter use. The oil would waterproof the skins, so after the stored food was gone, they would use the oil-soaked skins for waterproof maklaks, backpacks, and many other uses."

Siku can come and go from the lair through the breathing hole that she has made bigger. The ocean beneath the snow is home to all of the fish, shrimp, and other crustaceans that ringed seals eat.

If predators are near, the breathing hole doubles as an emergency exit to escape the lair quickly.

SEAL SCIENCE

Young ringed seals eat mostly small shrimp and other crustaceans.

Native Village of Kotzebue Environmental Program Director and coauthor Alex Whiting illustrated some of the most common crustaceans eaten by ringed seals.

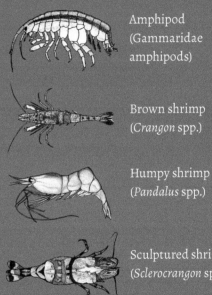

Amphipod (Gammaridae amphipods)

Brown shrimp (*Crangon* spp.)

Humpy shrimp (*Pandalus* spp.)

Sculptured shrimp (*Sclerocrangon* spp.)

Mysid (*Mysis* spp. and *Neomysis* spp.)

LIFE OF A LAIR

STEP 3: Once the ringed seal pup is born, she snuggles close to her mother to nurse. During early studies of ringed seals, scientists learned that a pup lair starts out as a single oval chamber that just fits the mother. Once the pup is born, the lair is slowly made bigger as the pup moves around in the lair and begins to tunnel into the walls of the snow cave around her.

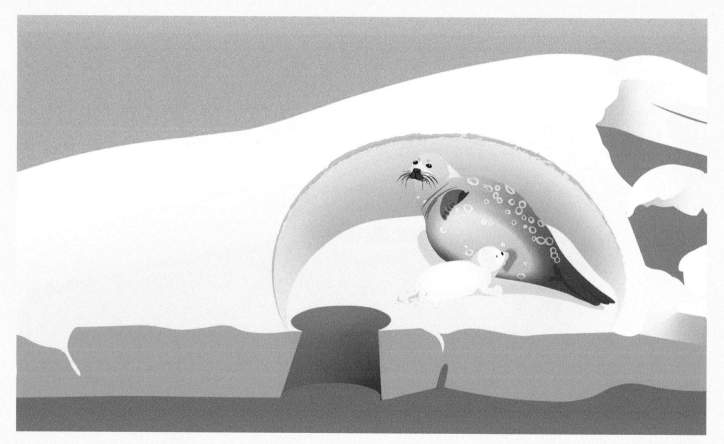

DRAWING BY HEATHER McFARLAND

NATCHIAYAAQ IS THE IÑUPIAQ
WORD FOR A WHITE RINGED
SEAL PUP.

SISI IS THE IÑUPIAQ WORD
FOR A RINGED SEAL LAIR.

Natchiq spends much of her pup life safe in the lair,
drinking milk from Siku and exercising her young muscles
as she grows fat and strong.

LIFE OF A LAIR

STEP 4: The pup explores her lair as she grows. She spends time digging new tunnels and making the lair larger while her mother is away looking for food.

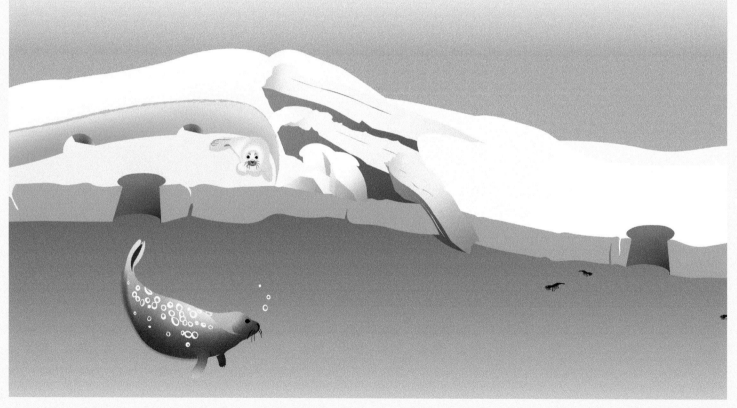

When Siku is out fishing, Natchiq digs into the sides of the snow cave, creating tunnels in the lair.

These small tunnels grow together and make more cozy rooms in Natchiq's lair.

The lair is growing as Natchiq grows.

SEAL SCIENCE

The average size of pup lairs found by the scientists working in Kotzebue Sound during 1983 was just over nine feet long with two or three rooms (about fifty-four square feet—or the size of an elevator). However, one lair was huge and measured a total of twenty-one feet long!

In 2019, scientists returned to Kotzebue Sound and studied ringed seal habitat with the Native Village of Kotzebue. Here they take measurements of an open seal lair.
DONNA D.W. HAUSER
(NOAA PERMIT 19309)

This pup is shedding its baby fur and growing its adult coat. By the time pups stop nursing they mostly have their adult coat. Their new blubber layer replaces their insulating coats.
KATHRYN J. FROST

A ringed seal pup with a thick fur coat, which it sheds by the time it stops nursing. Their new blubber layer replaces their insulating pup coat.
MICHAEL CAMERON (NOAA PERMIT 15126)

Within several weeks, Natchiq has grown a thick layer of fat, called blubber, to keep her warm in the cold ocean.

Siku shows her how to slide into the water through the breathing hole. Natchiq is a very good swimmer, even though she is still a pup!

INDIGENOUS KNOWLEDGE

Today almost every Iñupiaq household in Kotzebue eats seal oil. The high-calorie Omega-3-rich oil is eaten in many different ways:

✦ As a dipping sauce when eating aged frozen fish (*quaq*) and dried meat or fish (*paniqtaq*).
✦ As a condiment on cooked meat and fish or on raw fruits and vegetables.
✦ Poured into the hand-whipped caribou fat of "Eskimo ice cream" (*akutuq*).
✦ As a convenient trail food (*taquaq*) when combined with *paniqtaq*.

Blubber (uqsruġaaq) from ringed seals is rendered into easy-to-use oil.
ALEX V. WHITING

A pup peeking out of an open lair made in shallow snow in Kotzebue Sound, early April 2019.
JESSICA LINDSAY (NOAA PERMIT 19309)

Natchiq learns that there are lots of breathing holes scattered in the ice near her lair.

She surfaces at a new breathing hole, sucks in a breath, and goes back down to explore her underwater world.

Outside the safety of her lair, the world is large with much to explore.

INDIGENOUS KNOWLEDGE

Biologists worked with Qikiqtaġruŋmiut hunters and the Native Village of Kotzebue to learn about ringed seal behavior by working together to capture and tag seals.

Elder Cyrus Harris said, "As far as addressing the vision of the scientists, the local folks had a great technique for catching seals, so they used that method to accomplish their scientific goals. The overall results of what we documented from the tagged seals matched up with what we had known from our ancestors, but we backed it up with science."

LiFE OF A LAiR

STEP 5: A large ice pile caused snow to pile up on the downwind side. Her lair is dug in this deep hard-packed snowdrift. That makes it hard for predators and seal dogs to break or dig through the roof of her lair so that the pup has time to quickly escape through the breathing hole.

DRAWING BY HEATHER McFARLAND

Later that spring, Natchiq hears scratching on the roof of her lair. It is a fox-like animal with big ears that is digging and smelling her lair.

A seal dog.

Seal dogs help scientists find ringed seal lairs in the snow. The dogs can smell seals under the snow.

The lair might not be the safest place right now. Maybe the seal dog will dig through the snow ceiling?

Natchiq slides underwater through the breathing hole to get away from the seal dog.

SEAL SCIENCE

During the 1983 study, dogs were trained to find seal lairs. When a dog smelled a lair, it went to the location and began digging in the snow to show the scientists where it was.

Once a dog found a seal structure, the scientists measured the size of the lair or breathing hole and recorded snow and sea ice characteristics.

Pup lairs were found in deeper snow (nearly three feet) than simple adult lairs (about two feet five inches).

Charlie, a real-life seal dog, points to a ringed seal lair during the scientific research in Kotzebue in 1983.
KATHRYN J. FROST

John Goodwin (top).
SARAH BETCHER

John Goodwin holding a ringed seal during the Kotzebue Sound ringed seal tagging project (bottom).
KATHRYN J. FROST
(NOAA PERMIT 358-1787-02)

INDIGENOUS KNOWLEDGE: JOHN GOODWIN

John Goodwin, a Kotzebue Elder, grew up hunting ringed seals in Kotzebue Sound during the 1950s.

"One of the important things about ringed seals is they were always around, unlike caribou and other animals that may or may not be available from year to year.

"During mid-winter, it took hard work to find the resident seals. Not everyone would hunt, just a small number of experienced hunters would regularly go out. The local seals were pretty wild [skittish] and not easy to get. Not real high numbers either. Many times you could spend a couple hours or more trying to catch one seal. If you caught a couple or more seals in a day, that was a good catch, although at times after easterly winds, large leads could open up in the western sound, and many more seals might be taken.

"Later in the spring (April–May), when the young [subadult] ringed seals would show back up in the sound from their wintering grounds in the Bering Sea, the seals would be a lot more abundant, and many more hunters would go out. These seals caught in the late spring would be buried whole under the snow and out of the sun to be skinned out when it was warmer. They were made into *pokes* for storing seal blubber from the ringed seals and the spring *ugruk* [bearded seal] hunt. Before buckets were available, the skins from the pokes, after they were emptied of seal oil, would be cut up and made into small personal-sized backpacks to be used for berry picking. The backpacks were rectangular shaped, and a cloth or soft skin would be added to the top so the top could be tied shut to make sure the berries did not fall out."

Siku has built several getaway (or escape) lairs nearby. She is always prepared for predators like foxes and polar bears.

Each lair has a thick snow roof that makes it hard for predators (and seal dogs!) to dig through quickly.

When it snows in the winter, the roof gets thicker and stronger. This gives Natchiq and Siku more protection and more time to get away.

The snow on top of the lair is very important.

SEAL SCIENCE

Scientists working with Iñupiaq Elders from Kotzebue examined ringed seal pupping habitats during spring 2018 and 2019. The snow depths near lairs averaged about 12.5 inches.

In 1983, researchers measured snow depths averaging about thirty inches near ringed seal lairs. That's a big difference!

Scientists measured snow depths using an instrument called a magnaprobe, April 2019.
DONNA D.W. HAUSER
(NOAA PERMIT 19309)

Pup
tunnel

Breathing hole

A look through the open roof into a ringed seal
lair in Kotzebue Sound, April 2019. The lair has
a breathing hole to reach the surface and a small
tunnel into the wall made by a pup.
DONNA D.W. HAUSER (NOAA PERMIT 19309)

ANGAPAURAQ IS THE IÑUPIAQ
WORD FOR A YOUNG ADULT
RINGED SEAL.

UPINĠAKSRAQ IS THE IÑUPIAQ
WORD FOR SPRING.

Spring is coming. The air is getting warmer and the snow is getting softer. The ice and snow are melting.

The roof of Natchiq's lair gets thinner and a hole opens, where bright sun and warm air wash over the growing seal.

Lairs naturally melt away each spring when the warm weather comes. But the timing is critical.

Will Natchiq be grown-up enough to leave her lair and take care of herself before it melts away?

A hole opens in the lair as the spring sun warms and melts the lair's snow roof, and soon the entire lair will be open. Mother and the large pup bask in the spring sunlight next to their melting lair home.

DRAWING BY HEATHER McFARLAND

The lair does not provide much protection anymore. It has mostly melted away.

It is time for Natchiq to leave the place where she was born. Her pup lair is melted and gone.

Natchiq rests on top of the sea ice and basks in the brilliant spring sun in between bouts of diving and feeding nearby.

SEAL SCIENCE

Adult and juvenile ringed seals eat mostly fish.

Native Village of Kotzebue Environmental Program Director and coauthor Alex Whiting illustrated some of the most common fish eaten by ringed seals.

Arctic cod
(*Boreogadus saida*)
qaluaq

Saffron cod
(*Eleginus gracilis*)
uugaq

Pacific herring
(*Clupea pallasii*)
uqsruqtuuq

Rainbow smelt
(*Osmerus mordax*)
iḷhuaġñiq

In spring, cracks form in the melting ice. Seals bask on top of the ice near these cracks.
JESSICA LINDSAY (NOAA PERMIT 19309)

Natchiq and Siku spend a lot of time resting on the ice near breathing holes or cracks where they meet other seals and pups who were raised in the same area.

The ice is getting thinner.

In the summer, most of the ice will melt away, leaving a patchwork of floating ice floes in some areas.

A ringed seal swims in Kotzebue Sound.
JESSICA LINDSAY (NOAA PERMIT 19309)

Summer is here. It no longer gets dark at night as the sun sails across the Arctic sky. Even at midnight it is light enough for Natchiq to see predators far in the distance.

The sea ice has melted away along with Natchiq's pup lair. It is time for Natchiq to leave for good.

Siku encourages Natchiq to explore new waters and to journey north to spend the summer feeding.

Next winter the ocean will freeze again and form sea ice. In just a few years, Natchiq will dig out her own lair and have her own pup. Hopefully, there will be enough snow to dig a safe lair.

INDIGENOUS KNOWLEDGE

In 2007–2008, biologists worked with the Native Village of Kotzebue and Tribal members to attach satellite-linked tags to thirty-nine ringed seals.

The tags showed that in autumn, seals stay near the ice edge. Young seals traveled south into the Bering Sea as sea ice coverage expanded. They moved an average of twenty-two miles per day.

John Goodwin and his wife, Pearl, participated in the ringed seal capture and tagging efforts. John Goodwin discussed the research: "The seal tagging proved what our traditional knowledge knew about the seal migrations. Like we know certain size ringed seals, like the juveniles, show up here first from up north before the adults. With the tags, we learned the migration routes of the seals after they leave [Kotzebue] Sound."

Ringed seals are a primary prey species of polar bears in many parts of the Arctic, but polar bears are rare in Kotzebue Sound.
LLOYD PIKOK JR.

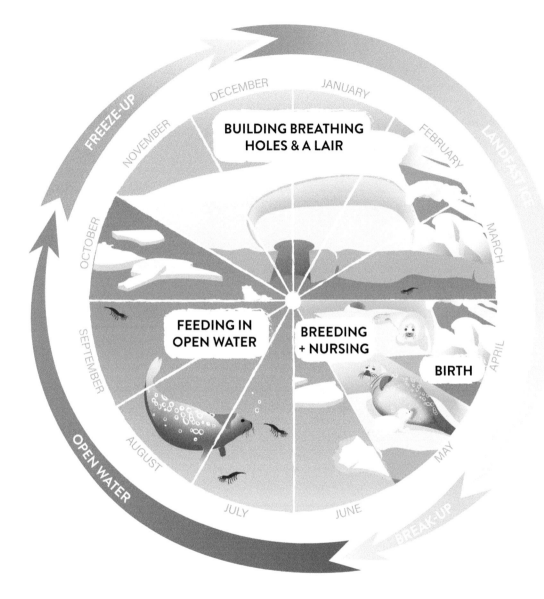

The activities of ringed seals are closely tied to the yearly cycle of sea ice.

DRAWING BY HEATHER McFARLAND

A YEAR IN THE LIFE OF A RINGED SEAL

To raise their pups, ringed seals need good ice platforms and snow cover to make lairs that will provide warmth and protection from predators. Because of this, the yearly life cycle of a ringed seal matches up closely with the yearly cycle of the Arctic ice.

FALL
In the autumn, the ocean starts to freeze, and the snow begins to fall. Ringed seals feed intensively at this time of year to put on weight for the long winter. The sea ice (*siku* in Iñupiaq) grows thicker and attaches to the shore, forming a stable platform known as landfast or shorefast ice (*tuvaq* in Iñupiaq). This stable landfast ice is where ringed seals prefer to have their pups.

WINTER
During long, dark, and stormy winters, snow builds up and drifts on the landfast ice. To breathe, ringed seals must either surface in cracks in the ice or through holes they make. Ringed seals are the only Arctic seals that regularly maintain breathing holes through the solid ice during winter. They use their teeth and front flipper claws to scrape the hole.

SPRING
Pups are born in the lairs dug into the snow by their mothers in spring. Pups nurse for 4-6 weeks before growing a thick blubber layer and a new coat of fur. Mating also occurs in the spring.

SUMMER
By early summer, the ice begins to melt (this is called "break-up"), and the seal pups must be ready to leave the lairs and survive on their own. There is usually no ice in the summer, except in the very far north. Seals may spend many days swimming and feeding.

INDIGENOUS KNOWLEDGE

In decades past, the Qikiqtaġruŋmiut could predict the yearly cycle of ice near Kotzebue.

Sea ice would usually be at its maximum in April and at its minimum in September. They knew what the ice would be like, and they could plan accordingly. But today the ice is less predictable.

Ice now freezes later in the fall, and the spring breakup is earlier and faster. The ice in winter is thinner.

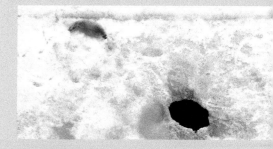

A ringed seal on very thin spring ice in May 2019.

JESSICA LINDSAY
(NOAA PERMIT 19309)

ABOUT THE AUTHORS

DONNA D.W. HAUSER is a Research Assistant Professor at the International Arctic Research Center at the University of Alaska Fairbanks, where she pursues interdisciplinary and collaborative research in marine ecology. She grew up on Dena'ina land in Anchorage, Alaska, where she sprouted her deep passion for Alaska's amazing people, places, and wildlife.

KATHRYN J. FROST worked as a Marine Mammals Research Biologist for the Alaska Department of Fish and Game from 1975 to 2000, studying the natural history and ecology of seals and beluga whales in Alaska. She studied the winter ecology of ringed seals in the Chukchi Sea and Kotzebue Sound in the 1980s and worked with the Native Village of Kotzebue Environmental Program beginning in 2003 to develop a community-based seal research program to satellite tag ringed and bearded seals in Kotzebue Sound.

ALEX V. WHITING developed the Environmental Program for the Native Village of Kotzebue in 1997. A major focus of the program has been Kotzebue Sound ecology, including marine mammal research. The approach of the Environmental Program has been to create partnerships between the Indigenous Knowledge Holders of the Tribe and outside researchers to undertake cooperative research efforts to understand the changing climate and the effects on the physical and natural environment of Kotzebue Sound.

JOHN GOODWIN is an Iñupiaq hunter who has lived in the Kotzebue area for more than fifty years and spent his entire life learning about the ocean and marine mammals of the area. He is an experienced commercial salmon fisherman and marine mammal hunter. John led field teams in catching and tagging bearded, spotted, and ringed seals in Kotzebue Sound from 2004 to 2015 and has participated in various Kotzebue Sound ecology research projects since 2002 with the Native Village of Kotzebue.

CYRUS HARRIS is an Iñupiaq hunter raised at Sisualik (a peninsula ten miles across Kotzebue Sound from Kotzebue) by his parents and grandparents. He grew up hunting, fishing, and living off the land and continues to live a subsistence lifestyle in his hometown. He currently is the Natural Resource Advocate for Maniilaq Association and manages the Hunter Support Program, which funds people in the region to hunt for traditional foods that will be served to Elders. He also maintains the traditional foods program facility (the *Siġḷuaq*) that provides traditional foods to the Elders residing at Kotzebue's Long-Term Care Facility. Cyrus led field teams in catching and tagging bearded, spotted, and ringed seals in Kotzebue Sound from 2004 to 2015 and has participated in various Kotzebue Sound ecology research projects since 2002 with the Native Village of Kotzebue.

PEARL GOODWIN is an Iñupiaq gatherer who grew up in Kiana on the Kobuk River but has lived in the Kotzebue area since 1970. She has traveled and lived out in the country extensively since she was a little girl. She spent years following her husband, John, hunting, trapping, and gathering. Pearl has assisted in catching and tagging bearded, spotted, and ringed seals in Kotzebue Sound from 2004 to 2015 and has participated in various Kotzebue Sound ecology research projects since 2002 with the Native Village of Kotzebue.

HEATHER McFARLAND translates complex scientific information about the Arctic, climate change, and wildlife populations into visual and written stories that people can understand. She is currently the Communications Lead at the International Arctic Research Center.

Pups become very independent and spend more time diving and looking for food when their lair melts away. The sea ice fractures as the weather warms and breaks into a puzzle of large ice floes with many places for the pups to rest.

DRAWING BY HEATHER McFARLAND

ACKNOWLEDGMENTS

This book would not have been possible without the generosity, hospitality, and patience of several individuals who have worked with and taught each of us so much about *natchiq* and the Iñupiaq way of life in Kotzebue and across coastal Arctic Alaska.

Combining Indigenous Knowledge with science to learn more about ringed seals has been the goal of the Native Village of Kotzebue and many Alaska seal biologists. By collaborating they wanted to learn more about seals' movements across the Bering and Chukchi Seas; their diving, hauling out, and feeding behavior; their site fidelity, and the genetics of different seal populations. Thanks to the efforts of many Kotzebue Elders, hunters, and residents, and together with biologists, more is known today about ringed seals in these areas than ever before. We would specifically like to acknowledge John Goodwin, Cyrus Harris, and Roswell Schaeffer Sr. for being leaders and partners on so much of our research. Other key partners in the Kotzebue region include Edward Ahyakak, Jeff Barger, Brenda Goodwin, Pearl Goodwin, Doc (Nereus) Harris III, Grover Harris, Grover Harris Jr., Lee Harris, Levi Harris, Jerry Jones, Boyuk (James) Monroe, and Robert Schaeffer.

We are grateful for the funding to produce this book from the North Pacific Research Board (Project no. 1811-90) and the Alaska Arctic Observatory and Knowledge Hub. The original 1983 project, "Winter Ecology of Ringed Seals in Alaska," was funded by the Minerals Management Service (now Bureau of Ocean Energy Management), US Department of the Interior, as part of the Outer Continental Shelf Environmental Assessment Program Research Unit 232. This was the subject of a project to "rescue" and publish these data funded by the North Pacific Research Board (Project no. 1811). The 2007–2009 study "Wintering Areas and Habitat Use of Ringed Seals in Kotzebue Sound, Alaska: a Community-Based Study" was funded by the Tribal Wildlife Grants Program of the Fish and Wildlife Service, US Department of the Interior, Anchorage, under Grant Number U-17-NA-1. Seals caught and tagged during this project were handled under Scientific Research Permit No. 358-1787, issued to the Alaska Department of Fish and Game. Research to study recent (2017–2020) spring sea-ice conditions, including ringed seal pupping habitats, was conducted as part of the Ikaaġvik Sikukun project funded by the Gordon and Betty Moore Foundation. We appreciate helpful reviews from Marilyn Sigman, Lori Quakenbush, and Deborah Bennett.

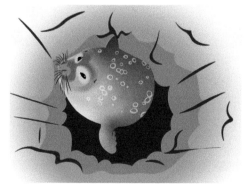

Special thanks to illustrator Heather McFarland for her work on the ringed seal lair graphics.